The
Iran-Contra
Scandal

CORNERSTONES OF FREEDOM
SECOND SERIES

Christine Petersen

Children's Press®
A Division of Scholastic Inc.
New York • Toronto • London • Auckland • Sydney
Mexico City • New Delhi • Hong Kong
Danbury, Connecticut

Photographs ©2004: AP/Wide World Photos: 3 (Dennis Cook), cover top (Lana Harris), 8 (Arturo Robles), 22, 30, 39; Corbis Images: 10 top, 19, 29, 44 top, 45 bottom left (Bettmann), cover bottom (Bill Gentile), 6 (MAPS.com), 28 (Wally McNamee), 35 (Louis Dematteis/Reuters NewMedia Inc.), 7 (Shepard Sherball), 11, 44 bottom left (Leif Skoogfors), 32 (Peter Turnley); Corbis SABA/Najlah Feanny: 18; Folio, Inc.: 13 (Michael Patrick), 38 bottom; Magnum Photos: 24 (Abbas), 5, 44 bottom right (Susan Meiselas); Panos Pictures/Paul Smith: 10 bottom, 45 top; PhotoDisc/Getty Images: 21; Robertstock.com: 9; Courtesy of Ronald Reagan Library: 27; The Image Works: 20 (Charles Bonnay), 15, 16, 17, 45 bottom right (John Nordell), 34 (Charles Steiner), 4 (Topham); Time Life Pictures/Getty Images: 12 (Terry Ashe), 40 (Dirck Halstead), 23 (Barry Iverson), 26 (Karl Schumacher), 31, 37 (Diana Walker), 14, 25.

Library of Congress Cataloging-in-Publication Data

Petersen, Christine.

   The Iran-Contra Scandal / Christine Petersen.

      p. cm. — (Cornerstones of freedom. Second series)

Summary: Discusses events leading up to the 1986 Iran-Contra scandal, wherein the Reagan administration sold guns to Iran in exchange for hostages and assisted rebels trying to overthrow the government of Nicaragua.

   Includes bibliographical references and index.

      ISBN 0-516-24228-8

      1. Iran-Contra Affair, 1985–1990—Juvenile literature. [1. Iran-Contra Affair, 1985–1990. 2. United States—Politics and government—1981–1989. 3. Iran—Politics and government—1979–1997. 4. Nicaragua—Politics and government—1979–1990.] I. Title. II. Series.

E876.P48 2004

973.927—dc22

                                      2003017614

1 2 3 4 5 6 7 8 9 10 R 13 12 11 10 09 08 07 06 05 04

O N NOVEMBER 25, 1986, President Ronald Reagan stood before dozens of reporters and television cameras in the White House pressroom. Two illegal government operations had been revealed during the previous month: the sale of weapons to Iran in exchange for the release of American hostages, and the assistance to rebels ("contras") who were trying to overthrow the government of Nicaragua. The president's part in these events had been questioned, and his public image was already severely damaged. It was with some nervousness that he faced the press once again.

General Anastasio Somoza (left) takes the oath as president of Nicaragua in 1955. After taking control of Nicaragua in 1937, he served as president until 1956, when he was assassinated.

REVOLUTION IN NICARAGUA

In 1937, General Anastasio Somoza took control of Nicaragua. For more than forty years, Somoza and his family ruled as Nicaragua's **dictators**, or absolute rulers. After becoming president in 1937, Somoza built up a powerful military, which took control of many public services, such as radio stations and the mail system, in order to control what people heard and said. Somoza and his friends became rich by buying up businesses and land all over the country. Meanwhile, the health-care and educational systems fell into ruin, so that many Nicaraguan people lived with hunger and disease. Year after year, elections were controlled to assure Somoza's victory. Anyone who dared to protest was put in prison or killed. By the late 1970s, many citizens of Nicaragua were angry and desperate.

In 1978, a revolutionary group called the Sandinista National Liberation Front took over Somoza's palace in Nicaragua's capital city of Managua. Claiming to seek a

On August 22, 1978, Sandinistas, disguised as members of the Nicaraguan military, stormed Somoza's palace. They held many government officials hostage.

CENTRAL AMERICA

Nicaragua is part of Central America, a thin ribbon of land tying together the two large continents of North America and South America. The region is home to seven countries: Guatemala, Belize, Honduras, El Salvador, Nicaragua, Costa Rica, and Panama. Nicaragua covers 49,579 square miles (128,410 square kilometers)—an area about the size of the state of New York—and is home to more than five million people. It is the largest—and the poorest—nation in Central America.

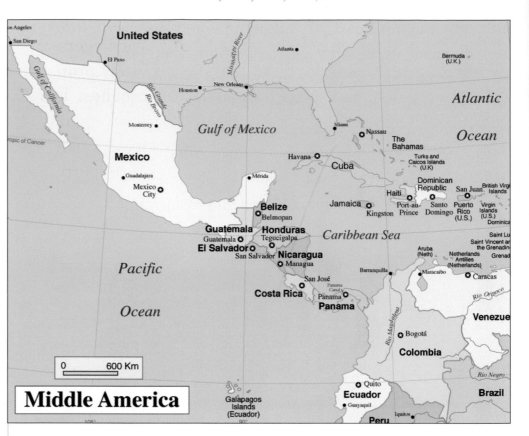

Nicaragua is part of Central America (also called Middle America), a region between the southern border of Mexico (North America) and the northwest border of Colombia (South America).

democratic government that would allow the Nicaraguan people to vote for their leaders and an economy in which all people would hold an equal share of the wealth, the Sandinistas won the support of many citizens. By the summer of 1979, they had taken power from the Somoza family.

It soon became clear, however, that the Sandinista government was no more democratic than the Somoza government had been. No elections were held—instead, five Sandinista

★ ★ ★ ★

military leaders took over the government. In order to "balance out" the country's wealth, many landowners and business owners were required to give up their property. The government now owned most farms, ranches, factories, and businesses, which were run by workers rather than by wealthy individuals. This approach is a form of **communism**, a political system in which all property and wealth are owned by the state.

A group of people in Managua wait in line to buy cheap bread. Poor planning by communist government leaders often led to food shortages.

The Sandinistas' commitment to communism soon became even more widespread. The new Nicaraguan leaders began to support communist **revolutionaries** in nearby El Salvador and to seek financial and military assistance from the powerful communist governments in the Soviet Union and Cuba.

For the average citizen of Nicaragua, this communist system wasn't all bad. Workers no longer had to depend on wealthy landowners and business owners for their survival, and many people began to receive the health care and education they had been deprived of under Somoza's

Nicaraguan president Daniel Ortega (right) talks with Cuban president Fidel Castro. Nicaraguan leaders sought assistance from other communist nations, such as Cuba.

President Harry Truman worked hard to convince the American people to resist communism.

THE TRUMAN DOCTRINE

After World War II, the spread of communism in Europe was a serious concern for America's leaders. In 1947, President Harry Truman proclaimed the Truman Doctrine, which declared that the United States would take a stand against communism throughout the world. "I believe that we must assist free peoples to work out their own destinies in their own way," Truman wrote. He believed that the United States should stand behind governments that supported democracy (the free election of governmental leaders by the people of a nation) and **capitalism** (the private ownership of goods and businesses), and that it should fight those that attempted to centrally control their economy or prevent the free election of leaders. For the next four decades, the Truman Doctrine influenced relationships between the United States and countries around the world. The fight against communism would lead to the Iran-contra scandal in the 1980s. The Truman Doctrine was not abandoned until 1991, after the fall of the Soviet Union's communist government.

Some Nicaraguans supported the Sandinistas. This photograph shows members of the Sandinista government waving to a cheering crowd in downtown Managua.

The contras, who banded together to fight the Sandinista government, were seen as "freedom fighters" by the United States government.

rule. Some Nicaraguans, however, resented this drastic change in their way of life. Former members of the Somoza government and people whose land or business had been taken over by the Sandinistas were especially unhappy. They began to form a group to fight the new government. The Nicaraguan Democratic Resistance, whose members were nicknamed "contras" (*contra* is the Spanish word for "against"), soon attracted the attention of the U.S. government.

AIDING THE CONTRAS

Alarmed by what he saw as an increase in communist activity around the world, United States president Ronald Reagan promised to work against communism after his election in 1980. Concerned that Nicaragua's Sandinista government would influence other Central American nations to embrace communism, one of his first decisions was to stop all financial assistance to the Sandinistas. Congress approved this plan, which the president said was to prevent the Sandinistas from sending weapons to communist groups in El Salvador.

President Reagan took his policy a step further: He authorized a program that allowed the Central Intelligence

This photograph of a protest march in El Salvador was taken in 1979, just before the outbreak of civil war. In an effort to prevent communism from taking hold there, the United States tried to control the flow of money and resources to the country.

★　　★　　★　　★

Agency (CIA) to provide **covert**, or secret, aid to the contras. Congress knew nothing of this plan and would not have approved it, but Reagan believed that it would help protect the American people from the threat of communism in Central America.

In November 1982, *Newsweek* magazine published a cover story suggesting that the CIA was helping the contras in their civil war against the Sandinista government in Nicaragua. Members of Congress were appalled that the policy they approved had secretly been changed to support the overthrow of another nation's government.

Representative Edward P. Boland, a Democrat from Massachusetts, spoke out angrily against providing aid to the contras. He and other congressional representatives

Edward Boland helped write the Boland Amendment, a law that prevented the president from supporting any activities to overthrow the Nicaraguan government.

The CIA provided military and financial support to the contras.

INTELLIGENCE

INTELLIGENCE

Most of us think of **intelligence** as the ability to learn facts and skills. For governments, intelligence takes on a deeper meaning. U.S. intelligence organizations such as the CIA gather information about the secret plans and activities of people, militaries, and governments around the world—especially those that could affect the security of the United States of America. These organizations also sometimes use covert activities to try to influence world events in ways that would benefit the United States.

quickly wrote a law that prevented the CIA and the Department of Defense from using federal money to overthrow the Nicaraguan government. Passed by a unanimous vote in the House of Representatives, the so-called Boland **Amendment** remained in effect until late 1984.

To get around the Boland Amendment, President Reagan signed a secret presidential order, called a **finding**, on September 19, 1983. The order stated that the United States would provide "support, equipment, and training" to the contras, but only for the purpose of encouraging the Sandinistas and Cuba to seek peaceful relationships with neighboring nations. Using this finding as an excuse, the CIA continued to provide military and financial support to the contras.

13

In April 1984, *Time* magazine—as well as several other publications— ran a story about the U.S. government's role in the Nicaraguan bombings.

In the spring of 1984, the *Wall Street Journal* reported that the CIA had helped the contras install mines (a kind of bomb) in the harbors of three Nicaraguan cities. The bombs were planted to keep other nations from sending supplies to the Sandinistas, and several ships were damaged when the mines exploded. Congress was once again outraged and decided to pass another law with stronger limits.

The second Boland Amendment made it clear that "the Central Intelligence Agency, the Department of Defense, or any other agency or entity of the United States involved in intelligence activities" was prohibited from using federal funds to aid the contras. With their funding gone, the Department of Defense and the CIA sent most of their staff back to the United States, leaving the contras without money or military advice.

THE NATIONAL SECURITY COUNCIL STEPS IN

Although Congress seemed to have written a law that completely stopped aid to the contras, President Reagan and his staff remained dedicated to the contra cause. The president turned to another government agency, the National Security Council (NSC), to take over the job of guiding the rebels.

The NSC is a group of advisers who work directly with the president to decide matters of national security and foreign policy. It is made up of senior federal government officials, including the president, the vice president, the secretary of state, and the secretary of defense. The national security adviser is responsible for managing the NSC staff, which carries out the day-to-day work of the council. In 1984, President Reagan told his national security adviser,

National Security Council staff worked closely with the president to secretly provide aid to the contras.

Robert McFarlane served as President Reagan's national security adviser.

★ ★ ★ ☆

Robert McFarlane, that the NSC staff was to "do whatever you have to do to help these people [the contras] keep body and soul together." The NSC staff was to do whatever was necessary to keep the revolutionary movement alive.

McFarlane ordered his assistant, Lieutenant Colonel Oliver North, to travel to Central America and meet with contra leader Adolfo Calero. Colonel North was a Marine Corps officer who had been assigned to the National Security Council staff in 1981. In 1983 he was part of a team that visited Central America in order to improve U.S. foreign policy in that region.

BODY AND SOUL

By the end of 1984, Colonel North had been put in charge of the operation to aid the contras. To help carry out the mission, North hired a staff of private citizens with experience in weapons sales and fund-raising.

One of the most important of these people was retired U.S. Air Force Major General Richard Secord. In the summer of

1984, North hired Secord and his business partner, Albert Hakim, to locate and buy weapons for the contras. Former CIA agent Thomas Clines joined the team as well. The threesome, who called themselves The Enterprise, set to work buying planes and hiring pilots to transport weapons to the contras. Secord and Hakim charged much more for the weapons than they paid, and they divided the profits between them.

As Colonel North secretly began his work in Central America, President Reagan met with his advisers to discuss a formal policy for aiding the contras. High on their list of topics was the idea of obtaining donations from other countries. Opinions about the plan were divided. CIA director William Casey encouraged the plan. Secretary of State George Shultz was against it because he had been advised that getting money from other countries without the approval of Congress was "an impeachable offense." In other words, the president could be brought to trial if the plan were discovered.

Lieutenant Colonel Oliver North would establish a secret network to arm the contras.

106TH CONGRESS—FIRST SESSION

United States Senate

Impeachment Trial of the
PRESIDENT OF THE UNITED STATES

JAN 07 1999 DATE

ADMIT BEARER TO THE SENATE GALLERY

Sergeant at Arms United States Senate

In American history, two presidents have been impeached—Andrew Johnson and Bill Clinton—but none have been removed from office. Shown here is a ticket to the Senate gallery, dated 1999, to witness the impeachment trial of President Clinton.

IMPEACHMENT

When a president or another senior government official is believed to have committed a crime, members of the House of Representatives may bring charges against him or her. This charge is called an **impeachment**. It is then the right of the Senate to hold a trial and vote on whether to remove the official from office.

Behind the scenes, the NSC staff was already looking for countries interested in giving money. For example, national security adviser McFarlane mentioned to Saudi Arabian leaders that the U.S. Congress had blocked aid to the contras and that the president would approve any support that helped keep the contra movement alive. The Saudis responded with an offer to donate one million dollars a month. After meeting with President Reagan in February 1985, the Saudi king increased his support to two million dollars a month.

To get the money to the contras, The Enterprise set up fake businesses and secret bank accounts in Switzerland.

18

Saudi Arabia deposited funds into this account every month, which North and Secord then gave to contra leaders in the form of weapons and supplies.

North also hired retired U.S. Army Major General John Singlaub to locate private citizens and additional countries that would be willing to contribute money to the contra cause. Singlaub was able to encourage Taiwan to contribute

President Reagan was able to continue supporting the contras with the help of Saudi Arabian leaders such as King Fahd, shown here.

one million dollars in 1985 and to give another one million dollars a few months later. Wealthy American citizens donated another ten million dollars to support President Reagan's fight against communism. Added to the Saudi contributions, donations totaled forty-four million dollars—enough to support the contras until Congress again approved money for their cause.

With so many nations and private individuals involved, the U.S. role in contra activities was not an easy secret to keep. Before long, news stories began to appear once again. The *Miami Herald* was on top of the story before anyone else. In late June 1985, the *Herald* reported that a U.S. agent had visited the contra base in Honduras and

The contras maintained a secret air base on the Honduras-Nicaragua border.

Capitol Hill was in a uproar after discovering the secret activities of the NSC.

had promised contra leaders that President Reagan would help them.

Other newspapers picked up the story several weeks later. Articles in the *New York Times* and the *Washington Post* in August 1985 caught the attention of officials in Washington—especially after the *Post* revealed the name of one of the players: Lieutenant Colonel Oliver North of the National Security Council staff.

The White House now had to deal with an angry Congress, which demanded an explanation of the NSC staff's activities. McFarlane was prepared with a denial. "I can state with deep personal conviction," he told Congress, "that at no time did I or any member of the National Security Council staff violate the letter or the spirit of the law." McFarlane claimed

KEEPING AN EYE ON CENTRAL AMERICA

Miami is located in southern Florida, less than 150 miles (241 kilometers) from Cuba and closer to Central America than any other city in the United States. For this reason, and because of the city's large Cuban American population, Miami's journalists pay close attention to political events in Central America and report them before most other American newspapers.

21

that the NSC staff had never asked for funds from other nations and that North had not provided any military advice to the contras.

McFarlane's lies convinced Congress that nothing illegal had taken place. Meanwhile, McFarlane, North, and the NSC staff continued their dealings with the contras.

MAKING DEALS WITH TERRORISTS

As events heated up in Nicaragua, another scandal was just beginning to brew far away, in Iran. Iran is located on the Persian Gulf, a desert region of the Middle East sandwiched

During the 1980s many terrorist activities were carried out against U.S. interests in the Middle East. This is a picture of the American embassy in Beirut, Lebanon (a Middle-Eastern city) after a bomb blast in April 1983.

between Africa and Asia. In the 1980s many Americans saw the Middle East as a hotbed of **terrorism** (kidnapping, bombing, and other activities carried out for political reasons).

In an attempt to prevent terrorism, President Reagan announced Operation Staunch in early 1984. Its goal was to discourage nations around the world from selling weapons to Iran. The president also made a strong statement against negotiating with terrorists, vowing that the United States would make no deals and pay no ransoms. "America will never make concessions to terrorists," he said, because "to do so would only invite more terrorism."

U.S. fears about terrorism in the Middle East were confirmed in March 1984 when Hizballah (also spelled Hezbollah), a militant Islamic group, took three Americans

Hizballah followed the teachings of the popular religious leader, Ayatollah Khomeini. Khomeini was believed to be one of the Middle East's strongest supporters of terrorist activities against the United States.

Hizballah, whose members generally oppose the Western world, is a major force in the Middle East. The name *Hizballah* means "party of God."

hostage in Beirut, Lebanon. Four more Americans were kidnapped in 1985. President Reagan's ideals were now put to the test. He had to decide whether to leave the hostages in Lebanon or to ignore his own policy in order to try to free them.

In the summer of 1985, an unexpected option for freeing the hostages came up. Israeli prime minister Shimon Peres sent representatives to talk with national security adviser Robert McFarlane. They told McFarlane that some Iranian leaders were interested in building a more peaceful relationship between Iran and the United States and might be able to free the seven American hostages in Lebanon. But there was one condition: The Iranians wanted to buy American-made missiles to use in their war with a neighboring nation, Iraq. Israel would sell the weapons to Iran, but Israel would need to buy replacements from the United States.

McFarlane immediately saw the risks. Not only did the plan go against Operation Staunch, but the Iranians might demand more and more weapons after the first shipment went through. Yet when he weighed this against the hope of bringing the hostages home, McFarlane decided it was a chance he was willing to take.

A few days later, President Reagan underwent surgery for colon cancer. While he was recovering, McFarlane visited him in the hospital and told him of Israel's offer. Anxious to see the hostages released, the president gave permission to open up talks with Iran. McFarlane contacted the Israelis and told them to make the sale.

TOW MISSILES

The weapons sent to Iran were called TOWS. TOWs are American-made missiles used to blow up tanks and other armored vehicles. They are usually mounted on top of cars or trucks. TOW missiles can hit targets as much as 2.3 miles (3.7 km) away, even in total darkness or during bad weather.

A U.S. soldier peers through the viewfinder of a TOW missile launcher.

On August 20, 1985, ninety-six TOW (antitank) missiles were delivered to Iran. An Iranian weapons dealer named Manucher Ghorbanifar represented the Iranians in the deal. He told McFarlane that the Iranians could arrange to have one hostage released in exchange for the missiles. McFarlane picked CIA agent William Buckley but was told that Buckley was too sick to travel. No other hostages were released in Buckley's place.

A few weeks later, Ghorbanifar informed McFarlane that the Iranians could convince Hizballah to release one hostage if 400 more TOWs were delivered. Despite the failure of the first sale, 408 TOWs were shipped from Israel in September 1985. On the day of their arrival, hostage Reverend Benjamin Weir was released. McFarlane ordered Colonel Oliver North to make arrangements to bring the minister home.

Reverend Benjamin Weir was released eighteen months after he was taken hostage.

HOOKED

In November 1985, Colonel North contacted Richard Secord and asked him to set aside his work in Nicaragua for a while to supervise the shipment of more weapons to Iran.

Because of Operation Staunch, no country was supposed to be selling weapons to Iran. North knew that the weapons would have to be shipped secretly and that the real nature of the cargo would have to be disguised. He solved this problem by asking for help from the CIA. North claimed to be sending oil-drilling parts to Iran, and said he wanted the name of a privately owned airline that the CIA used to covertly send agents and deliveries around the world. Using this airline, North and Secord shipped eighteen HAWK antiaircraft missiles to Iran.

This created another problem. By law, an order from the president was required before CIA resources could be used by other government agencies. The CIA's attorney quickly drew up a presidential finding and gave it to President Reagan to sign. This finding was the first official document that proved the United States was involved in selling weapons to Iran in exchange for hostages.

Despite the obstacles that had already arisen in the Iran weapons deal, President Reagan remained as devoted to the idea of freeing the hostages as he was to aiding the contras. Reagan's advisers, however, were split in their opinions. Secretary of State George Shultz and Secretary of Defense

In December 1985 and January 1986, the president held several meetings with his most important advisers about the Iran weapons deal.

★　★　★　★

Attorney General Edwin Meese became directly involved in the Iran-contra scandal after providing legal advice to the president.

Caspar Weinberger were strongly opposed to continuing any weapons deals with Iran. By contrast, CIA director Casey and new national security adviser Admiral John Poindexter (who replaced Robert McFarlane in late 1985) wanted to set up more weapons shipments in hopes that this would lead to the release of more hostages. President Reagan was the deciding voice: As long as hope remained for more Americans to come home, the operation would continue.

One major roadblock to the deal was the Arms Export Control Act. The act said that American weapons could not be sold to countries that supported terrorism, and it required that Congress be notified if any such sales took place. The government's top lawyer, Attorney General Edwin Meese III, offered a solution. The National Security Act was another law that dealt with the sale of weapons. This law could be used to authorize the sale, Meese said, if the president would sign a finding stating that the weapons were sold to protect the United States.

President Reagan signed a finding on January 17, 1986. Later that day he wrote in his diary, "I agreed to sell TOWs

low internists of terrorism. You have discussed the general
outlines of the Israeli plan with Secretaries Shultz and
Weinberger, Attorney General Meese and Director Casey. The
Secretaries do not recommend you proceed with this plan.
Attorney General Meese and Director Casey believe the short-term
and long-term objectives of the plan warrant the policy risks
involved and recommend you approve the attached Finding. Because
of the extreme sensitivity of this project, it is recommended
that you exercise your statutory prerogative to withhold
notification of the Finding to the Congressional oversight
committees until such time that you deem it to be appropriate.

Recommendation

OK   NO

RR   _   That you sign the attached Finding.

Prepared by:
Oliver L. North

Attachment
    Tab A - Covert Action Finding

1100 17 Jan 8.

President was briefed verbally from this paper
VP, Don Regan and Don Fortier were present.

This is a copy of the finding stating that weapons were sold to protect the United
States. It was signed by the president on January 17, 1986.

to Iran." This short sentence summed up a huge decision.
Up to this point, Israel had conducted all weapons sales
to Iran; the United States merely provided replacements
afterward. The United States was now committed to selling weapons directly to Iran in exchange for the release of
the hostages.

★ ★ ★ ★

USING THE PROFITS

The plan was simple. The CIA would buy missiles from the U.S. Department of Defense. Secord would collect money from Iran, buy the missiles from the CIA, and ship the weapons to Iran. As a private businessman, Secord charged the Iranians much more for each missile than he paid the U.S. government. The profits—more than two thousand dollars per missile—went into The Enterprise's Swiss bank account instead of to the U.S. government. Secord managed the money, but Colonel North made all decisions about how it was spent.

The scandal could not have been carried out without the knowledge of the Department of Defense. The Pentagon, shown below, is the Department of Defense headquarters in Arlington, Virginia.

John Poindexter later said that he chose not to ask for the president's approval in order to protect Reagan from being held responsible if the story ever came out.

At a meeting in late January 1986 in London, Ghorbani-far took Colonel North aside and suggested that some of the profits from the weapons sales could be used to support the Nicaraguan contras. When North brought the idea to his boss, national security adviser John Poindexter, Poindexter was enthusiastic. Believing that President Reagan would approve, Poindexter authorized the plan, possibly without talking to the president first. In February 1986,

David Jacobsen hugs a family member after his release.

* * * *

Secord delivered one thousand TOW missiles to Iran in two shipments. In May, 240 spare parts for antiaircraft missiles were sent. That same month, former national security adviser McFarlane and Colonel North led a group to Tehran, the capital of Iran, in a secret effort to make a deal that would free all of the hostages. The meetings went poorly, and once again no hostages were released.

Iran finally appeared to hold up its end of the bargain by arranging for the release of two hostages: the Reverend Lawrence Jenco in late July 1986 and David Jacobsen in early November. Yet it became more and more clear that Iran did not have control over the kidnappers. In September, two more Americans, Frank H. Reed and Joseph Cicippio, were taken hostage in Beirut. Even after this setback, another shipment containing five hundred TOWs went out in October. The profits totaled more than sixteen million dollars, about four million of which went to the contras.

THE GAMES ARE REVEALED

While he organized the weapons sales to Iran in the spring of 1986, Colonel North again began to receive attention from the press. The *Miami Herald* ran a story revealing the activities of the NSC staff in Central America. Throughout the spring and summer, the *Herald* reported the details of North's role in providing money, supplies, and military advice to the rebels. In June television reporters took up the story.

The scandal began to receive media attention in the spring of 1986.

Members of Congress demanded information. Poindexter repeatedly refused to help them, stating only that the NSC staff had broken no laws. He did, however, allow Congress to speak to North. In August a committee interviewed the colonel, who said that his involvement with the contras had merely been to help them get more support from the Nicaraguan people. Taking North at his word, the committee members were relieved and let the matter drop.

But the story did not die. On October 5, 1986, Sandinista soldiers shot down a contra supply plane containing ammunition and weapons. Only one person survived: a former U.S. Marine named Eugene Hasenfus, who was part of North and Secord's secret network. The Sandinistas captured Hasenfus a day after the crash and put him on international television. He admitted to the world that the United States had been secretly providing the contras with weapons and supplies.

Panic set in among those government officials who knew about the contra supply operation. Casey and North agreed to stop the contra operation, and North began to shred reports, orders, and financial documents that might provide evidence of their activities.

Weapons sales to Iran continued through October, but this operation, too, was about to fall apart. That month angry students in Tehran dropped five million leaflets onto the city, revealing that McFarlane and North had met with

Nicaraguans lead an American prisoner, Eugene Hasenfus, through the jungle. His captors placed him on world television, where he admitted the truth about the scandal.

Iranian representatives there. The students were outraged that their nation's leaders had been cutting secret deals with a nation they claimed to hate. A Lebanese newspaper, *Al-Shiraa*, went further by announcing that the goal of these meetings had been to conduct a weapons deal, despite the official ban of the United States on weapons sales to Iran.

Two weeks later, on November 13, President Reagan went on television to speak to the nation. He stated that the Tehran meetings had been an effort to promote peace with Iran and to arrange for the hostages to be freed. "We did not—repeat—did not trade weapons or anything else for hostages, nor will we," he declared. But the American people were doubtful. Newspaper and White House polls showed that only one person in seven believed the story. The situation was made worse a week later when the president took part in a live question-and-answer session with the press. Here he restated his claim that the United States had not participated in weapons sales. Unfortunately, his chief of staff had already admitted the sales in another interview.

In an effort to clarify what had taken place, the president gave Attorney General Meese three days to investigate the situation. Meese ordered two of his lawyers to search for evidence. Poindexter had already torn up the finding that proved President Reagan had approved the sale of weapons to Iran in November 1985 in exchange for hostages. Colonel North also thought he had shredded anything that would prove the scandal.

President Reagan spoke to the American public about the scandal in a televised speech.

But North had missed one important item. While searching the colonel's office, the attorneys were shocked to find a report written by North in April 1986. In this report, North clearly stated that the United States had willingly sold weapons to Iran in exchange for hostages. Worse yet, he revealed a plan in which millions of dollars in profits from the weapons sales, rather than being paid to the U.S. government, would be secretly held aside and sent to Nicaragua to support the contras.

THE INVESTIGATIONS

On November 25, 1986, President Reagan again stood before the press. He announced that Oliver North had been removed from the NSC staff and that national security adviser John Poindexter had resigned. Attorney General Meese then stepped up to the microphone to tell the story of the newly discovered connection between the NSC's activities in Iran and Nicaragua.

Attorney General Edwin Meese appeared on television to talk about his findings related to the scandal.

Robert McFarlane (standing left) faced a wall of photographers and congressional representatives during the first week of hearings on the Iran-contra scandal.

President Reagan immediately appointed former senator John Tower to oversee an inspection of the NSC staff. He also ordered that an independent lawyer be hired to look into the Iran and contra operations. The Senate and the House of Representatives announced their own investigations.

Congressional hearings went on for forty days in 1987. Throughout the hearings, participants in the Iran-contra scandal repeatedly lied to protect themselves, their coworkers, and the president. Once they were forced to tell the truth, many defiantly said that they were proud of their involvement. NSC staff members also admitted that President Reagan authorized the operations in Iran and Nicaragua, although no evidence was ever found that he knew about the use of profits from weapons sales to help the contras.

39

In March 1988, John Poindexter, Oliver North, Richard Secord, and Albert Hakim were charged with twenty-three crimes against the United States. Robert McFarlane and nine other officials were charged and later convicted on lighter charges, many of which were pardoned by President George H. W. Bush in 1992. Poindexter and North were found guilty of various crimes but the charges were later overturned because Congress had promised the men that their testimonies would not be used against them. No charges were brought against President Reagan, whose public image recovered quickly. By the end of his presidency in 1988, Reagan was considered one of the most popular presidents of the twentieth century.

RESPECTING THE LAW

When the Constitution was written, its authors divided the responsibility of government among three groups, or

By the end of the scandal, Reagan was portrayed as being confused and "kept in the dark" about what was really going on. He remains one of our most popular presidents.

branches—the executive (presidential), the legislative (congressional), and the judicial (the courts). Each of these branches has separate powers to act as "checks and balances." But the Constitution also requires that the executive and legislative branches work together to make decisions that affect our relationships with other nations. For example, the president commands the army and navy, appoints ambassadors to other nations, and speaks for the United States when treaties are being negotiated. Congress has the option to veto ambassadors that the president chooses. It declares war and provides money to support the military. Congress also controls trade between the United States and other nations and gives final approval on treaties.

During the long investigation of the Iran-contra affair, one thing became clear: Everyone involved believed he or she was doing the right thing. President Reagan and the NSC staff sought to protect the American people from the spread of communism, and they wanted to free the American hostages. These seem like admirable goals. But our Constitution does not allow a few people to make important decisions that affect the security and welfare of all Americans. Nor does it allow anyone to break the law, even if their goals appear to be worthy. Members of Congress were elected to speak on behalf of the country's citizens, and any action taken without their approval—even if ordered by the president—defies the heart of our democracy. The Iran-contra scandal reminds us that our government works only when everyone respects its laws.

Glossary

amendment—an addition to a bill written by Congress

capitalism—an economic system in which goods and businesses are owned by private individuals

communism—a political system in which all property and wealth are owned by the government

covert—secret

dictators—government leaders who control a country by force

finding—an order signed by the president authorizing a covert action

impeachment—criminal charges brought against a government official

intelligence—information gathered by a government for political, military, or other policy purposes

revolutionaries—people seeking to make major changes to a government, usually by overtaking the government rather than by election

terrorism—kidnapping, bombing, and other activities carried out for political reasons

Timeline: The Iran-

1979	1981	1982	1983	1985		1986

1979

JULY
Sandinista National Liberation Front takes over the government of Nicaragua.

1981

FEBRUARY
Reagan administration stops all aid to the Nicaraguan government.

· · · · · · · · ·

DECEMBER
Reagan authorizes covert support for the contras.

1982

DECEMBER
First Boland Amendment, intended to ban funding of the contras through late 1984, passes.

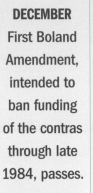

1983

MARCH–APRIL
Operation Staunch seeks an international ban on arms sales to Iran.

· · · · · · · · ·

DECEMBER
Second Boland Amendment passes, strengthening the ban on aid to the contras through September 1985.

1985

AUGUST–SEPTEMBER
U.S. authorizes Israel to make the first deliveries of TOW missiles to Iran.

· · · · · · · · ·

SEPTEMBER 15
Hostage Benjamin Weir is released.

NOVEMBER
A shipment of HAWK missiles is sent to Iran.

1986

JANUARY–OCTOBER
Arms and spare parts continue to be delivered to Iran.

Contra Scandal

1988

JANUARY 17
President Reagan signs finding authorizing the United States to sell weapons directly to Iran in exchange for hostages.

JULY 26
Hostage Lawrence Jenco is released.

SEPTEMBER
Two more Americans are taken hostage.

OCTOBER 5
Eugene Hasenfus is captured In Nicaragua after his plane, carrying supplies to the contras, is shot down by Sandinistas. The shoot-down exposes the secret U.S. supply program to the contras.

NOVEMBER 2
Hostage David Jacobsen is released.

NOVEMBER 3
Lebanese news magazine *Al-Shiraa* reports on U.S.-Iran weapons deals.

MID-NOVEMBER
President Reagan makes a television speech to explain the Iran weapons deals, but his remarks increase public doubt.

NOVEMBER 22
Report detailing the use of profits from Iran arms sales to support contras is found in Oliver North's office.

NOVEMBER 25
Reagan announces the firing of Oliver North and the resignation of John Poindexter. The president and Congress later order investigations of arms sales and aid to the contras.

North, Poindexter, Secord, and Hakim are found guilty of crimes relating to the Iran-contra scandal. McFarlane and nine other officials are sentenced

on lighter charges. Several defendants' sentences are later overturned on legal technicalities. Others are pardoned by President George H. W. Bush.

To Find Out More

BOOKS AND VIDEOS

Greenblatt, Miriam. *Iran*. Danbury, CT: Franklin Watts, 2003.

Klingel, Cynthia, and Robert B. Noyed. *Ronald Reagan: Our Fortieth President*. Chanhassen, Minn.: Child's World, 2002.

Morrison, Marion. *Nicaragua*. Danbury, CT: Franklin Watts, 2002.

ONLINE SITES

CIA's Homepage for Kids
http://www.cia.gov/cia/ciakids/index.shtml

Hizballah (Party of God)
http://library.nps.navy.mil/home/tgp/hizbalah.htm

Nicaragua—A Country Study
http://lcweb2.loc.gov/frd/cs/nitoc.html

World Almanac for Kids—Iran
http://www.worldalmanacforkids.com/explore/nations/iran.html

Index

Bold numbers indicate illustrations.

About the Author

Christine Petersen is a middle-school teacher who lives near Minneapolis. She has also worked as a biologist studying the natural history and behavior of North American bats. In her free time, Christine enjoys snowshoeing, canoeing, bird-watching, and writing educational books for young people. She is a member of the Society of Children's Book Writers and Illustrators and is the author of more than a dozen Children's Press books.